SPEAK OUT 1

David Nunan

Thomson Asia Pte Ltd

Singapore • Albany • Belmont • Bonn • Cincinnati • Detroit • Johannesburg
London • Madrid • Melbourne • Mexico City • New York • Paris • Tokyo • Toronto

First published 1999 by:
International Thomson Asia ELT
60 Albert Street
#15-01 Albert Complex
Singapore 189969

The publication of *Speak Out: Book One* was directed by the International Thomson Asia ELT Team:

- Karen Chiang, *ELT Director*
- Christopher Wenger, *Senior Development Editor*
- Joan Quick, *Development Editor*
- Teri Tan, *Production Editor*
- Connie Wai, *Production Co-ordinator*
- Julian Thomlinson, *ELT Consultant*

Designed by Raketshop Design Studio, Philippines

- Leo Cultura, *Creative Director*
- Ibarra Crisostomo, *Designer*
- Glen Giron, Jomar Soriano, Jane Legazpi, Roel Cancio, Joseph Estrada, *Illustrators*
- Donna Guerrero, Erick John Elayda, *Computer Artists*
- Luthy Pasamonte, *Copy Editor*

Printed by Chong Moh Offset Printing Pte Ltd, Singapore

1 2 3 4 5 03 02 01 00 99
ISBN 0-534-83560-0

AUTHOR'S ACKNOWLEDGEMENT

This series has been a joy to write, and it has been a joy because of the very special people I have had the privilege to work with throughout its development. To Bob Cullen, who, having heard me speak English, still thinks I can teach it to others; to Karen Chiang, whose knowledge, clarity of vision, and friendship I value so highly; to Chris Wenger, who never ceases to astonish me with his extraordinary gift as an editor; to Leo Cultura, Ibarra Crisostomo and the other creative artists at Raketshop Design Studio, I can only say that your illustrations and designs gave me inspiration; and to Joan, Julian, Teri, and Connie — you all know the unique contribution you had to this project. I hope that my heartfelt "thank you" means as much to you as your dedication and commitment mean to me.

In addition to the above, I would like to extend my thanks to the following professionals who have offered invaluable comments and suggestions during the development of this series:

CANADA
- Wilma Nederend, Vancouver Community College

JAPAN
- Lesley D. Riley, Kanazawa Institute of Technology
- Nan Y. Hiraiwa, Tokai University
- John Thomson, Fujimura Joshi High School

KOREA
- David Bohlke, University of Seoul
- Ellen Ko, University of Seoul
- Ho Hahn, Sejong University

TAIWAN
- Ann-Marie Hadzima, National Taiwan University
- Megan Montgomery, National Taiwan University
- Wesley Hsi, Ministry of Personnel, Examination Yuan, ROC

PHOTO CREDITS

The ELT Editorial Team of International Thomson Publishing Asia would like to thank the following embassies and tourist boards in Singapore for the use of their extensive photo libraries for *Speak Out: Book One*:

- Singapore Tourism Board... *p.67*
- Italy Cultural Institute... *p.97*

Special thanks to friends and colleagues of ITP Asia for sharing their photographs with us and for adding to the ITP Asia Photo Collection.

CONTENTS

Scope & Sequence

Unit	Title	Goals	Target Language	Pronunciation
1	Are you Dr. Lowe?	• Introducing yourself • Practicing greetings • Asking who people are	• My name is Ron. • What's your name? • Are you Julie?	Question and statement intonation
2	Is that your family?	• Talking about your family • Asking about families	• Is that your family? • Yes, these are my parents. • Do you have any brothers or sisters?	Pronouncing *th*
3	Do you know Amy?	• Asking about appearance • Describing others • Expressing uncertainty	• Do you know George? • I'm not sure. What does he look like? • Is he tall? Does he have short hair?	Reduced speech in sounds connecting words
4	Do you speak English?	• Asking for and offering help • Thanking people • Describing locations	• Do you speak English? • Can I help you? • Thank you. • Where's the hotel, please? • It's next to the bank.	Vowel sounds
5	Where are you from?	• Asking and answering questions about where people are from	• Where are you from? • I'm from Canada. • Are you on vacation? • What do you do?	Syllable stress
6	Make yourself at home.	• Welcoming someone • Offering, accepting and refusing	• Come in. Make yourself at home. • Would you like some coffee? • May I have some water?	Pronouncing *c* as /s/ or /k/
7	How much is this sweater?	• Asking about and stating prices • Talking about forms of payment	• How much is it? It's $16. • I'll take this shirt. • That'll be $30, please. • Do you take credit cards?	Rising intonation for confirmation
8	I need a part-time job.	• Expressing desires • Making suggestions • Talking about likes and dislikes	• What kind of job do you want? • I want to work as a lifeguard. • Why don't you try Sunshine Pools? • Yes, I'm a waiter.	Sentence stress patterns
9	Is there a pool?	• Asking for and identifying locations in a building • Giving directions	• Excuse me. Is there a pool in this hotel? • How do I get there? • Take the stairs to the second floor.	Stress for information focus
10	First, you turn it on.	• Describing procedures • Narrating a sequence	• Do you know how to use a computer? • I can't turn on the VCR. • First, you need to plug it in.	Pronouncing /s/ and /sh/

Unit	Title	Goals	Target Language	Pronunciation
11	I get up early.	• Describing routines and schedules • Telling time	• What's the matter? • Why are you tired? • What time do you get up? • I get up at 5:30 every morning.	Intonation to transform statements into questions
12	I'd like a hamburger.	• Ordering food and drink • Asking for additional information	• Can I help you? • I'd like an iced tea, please. • What size would you like? Is that all?	Pronouncing /s/ and /z/
13	Do you like basketball?	• Talking about likes and dislikes • Describing sports	• Do you like golf? • No, not really. It's boring. • What sports do you like?	Syllable stress
14	Do you want to see a movie?	• Inviting • Making excuses	• Do you want to see a movie? • What's playing? • How about a science fiction movie? • Sorry, I have to work late.	Intonation to show surprise
15	What's the weather like?	• Talking about the weather • Making suggestions	• What's the weather like? • It's hot and sunny. • Let's go on a picnic tomorrow. • What's the weather going to be like?	Stress for information focus
16	What can we get him?	• Talking about what people like • Talking about gift giving	• What can we get her? • How about getting her a CD? • No, she already has a lot of CDs. • What do you like doing?	Pronouncing *What's...* and *What does...* in reduced speech
17	We should go to the beach.	• Making suggestions • Voicing objections	• Where should we go on vacation? • What can we do there? • We can go swimming. • I don't like swimming.	Pronouncing *can* and *can't*
18	What's she like?	• Describing qualities of people and jobs • Using degrees of description	• What's she like? • She's really nice. • How's your new job? • It's kind of boring.	Question and statement intonation
19	What do you think of the class?	• Asking about opinions • Expressing preferences • Agreeing and disagreeing	• What do you think of the class? • It's great. I like group work. • I do too. • Not me. I like studying alone.	Word stress for emphasis
20	I lost my cell phone.	• Talking about what you did and who you met • Asking about past events	• I lost my cell phone. • Where did you go today? • First, I went to the bank. • What did you do there?	Vowel sounds

GOALS

Are you Dr. Lowe?

- Introducing yourself
- Practicing greetings
- Asking who people are

Get Ready

Write the response in the correct place below.

Nice to meet you, Rick. | Yes, I am. | No. I'm not. I'm Dr. Harris.

Check your answers.

Start Talking

Number the lines of the conversation in the correct order.

_____ No, I'm not. I'm Mary.

_____ Are you Pat?

_____ Nice to meet you, Mary. I'm Ron.

Practice with a partner.

Practice with your classmates. Use your own name.

Listen In

Listen and check (✓) the expressions every time you hear them.

- [ ] Excuse me.
- [ ] Are you...?
- [ ] Yes, I am.
- [ ] No, I'm not.
- [ ] Nice to meet you.
- [ ] What's your name?

Listen again and number the names you hear (1-4).

Bill	Mr. Mendoza	Mr. Sanders
Melinda	Larry Stevens	Tina Jones

Say It Right

Listen to the example.

Are you Susan?
No, I'm not.

Is the intonation rising (↗) or falling (↘)? Listen and mark the intonation.

Excuse me.
Are you Melinda?
Yes?
Yes, I am.

I'm Bill.
Nice to meet you.

Listen again and practice.

Talk Some More

Number the sentences to make a conversation (1-6).

6 Julie Martin.
Nice to meet you, Kevin.
I'm Kevin Tanner.
Hi.
What's your name?
1 Hello.

Check your answers.

Practice the conversation with a partner. Use your own information.

Work In Pairs

Ask your partner for the missing names. Fill in the blanks.

Student A Student B go to page 81.

BACK ROW : Lisa Maxwell, __________, Carla Diaz, Roger Walker
FRONT ROW : __________, Eric Simmons, __________

What's his name?
Roger Walker.
How do you spell that?

Speak Out

Ask for your classmates' names.
Fill in the list.

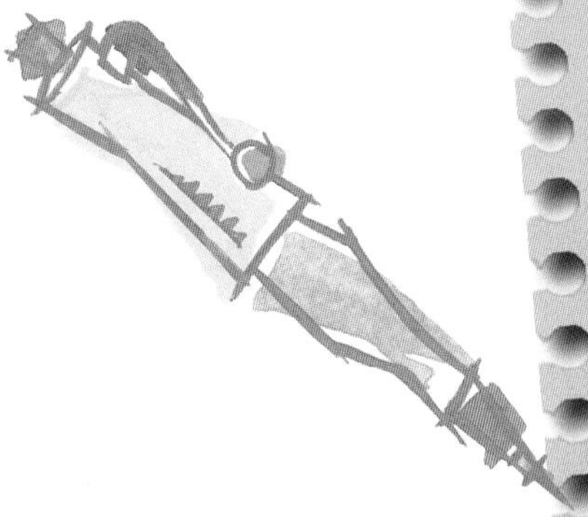

CLASS LIST

Answer the questions. Check with a partner.

Does anyone in your class have the same family name?	☐ Yes	☐ No
Does anyone in your class have the same first name?	☐ Yes	☐ No
What is the longest family name in your class?	________	
What is the shortest family name in your class?	________	

ZOOM IN

What do you usually say when you...

- want to call a waiter's attention?
- want to ask a stranger a question?
- accidentally step on someone's foot in a crowd?
- want someone to move out of your way?

In English, people usually say *Excuse me.* In what kinds of situations do you usually say this?

GOALS

Is that your family?

- Talking about your family
- Asking about families

Get Ready

Write the words next to the correct people.

mother, father, son, daughter, brother, sister, husband, wife

Is that your family?
Yes, it is. This is my husband.
Are those your children?
Yes. This is my son and this is my daughter.
Mother
Wife
Daughter
Mother
Wife

Start Talking

Look at the conversation above.

Practice with a partner.

Look at the family above.
Imagine this is your family. Take turns asking and answering questions with a partner.

Is that your mother?

Listen In

Listen and check (✓) the words you hear.

☐ father	☐ mother	☐ husband	☐ wife	☐ children
☐ brother	☐ daughter	☐ sister	☐ son	☐ parents

Listen again and find Joe's family.

Say It Right

Write the letter next to the correct sentence.

☐ This is my daughter.

☐ This is my father.

☐ These are my children.

☐ This is my mother.

Listen and check your answers.

Listen again and practice. Pay attention to the pronunciation of *th*.

Talk Some More

Write the words in the correct spaces.

I	have
you	do

Do _______ have any brothers or sisters?

_____ have two sisters.

Yes, I _______. I _______ a brother and two sisters. How about you?

Practice with a partner. Use your own information.

Work In Pairs

Student A

Student **B** ☞ go to page 82.

Imagine you're one of the people in this family. Answer your partner's questions.

Ask your partner questions. Draw his/her family tree.

Do you have any children?

Speak Out

Ask your classmates questions.
Find someone who...

Do you have any brothers or sisters?

	NAME
has a sister	
has two brothers	
has a brother and a sister	
has more than three brothers or sisters	
is an only child	
has one child	
has three children	

Work in groups. Compare your answers. Then answer these questions:

Who has the most brothers in your group?	
Who has the most sisters in your group?	
Who has the most children in your group?	

Share your answers with the class.

ZOOM IN

In some cultures, it is impolite to ask "Are you married?" when meeting for the first time, but in other cultures, it's all right.

Are you married?

How about in your culture? When can you usually ask this question?

Do you know Amy?

- Asking about appearance
- Describing others
- Expressing uncertainty

Get Ready **Write the numbers in the correct places in the picture (1-10).**

Do you know Amy?
I don't know. What does she look like?
She's kind of short, and she has curly hair.
Oh, yes. I know her.
ERIK
SANDRA
AMY
TONY
KATHI
GEORGE

1. tall
2. young
3. blond hair
4. curly hair
5. short
6. middle-aged
7. glasses
8. short hair
9. large earrings
10. mustache

Do you know George?

Start Talking

Look at the conversation above.

Practice with a partner.
Talk about the other people above.

Listen In

Listen and match the name with the correct person.

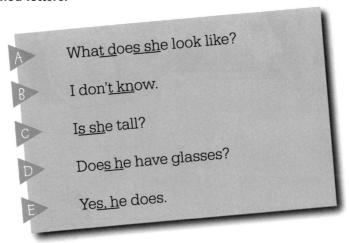

Brian Morgan

Nina Hansen

Michael Shea

Annie Jones

Listen again. Check (✓) the names of the people the speakers *know.*

Say It Right

Some sounds are not pronounced clearly in rapid speech. Listen and pay attention to the underlined letters.

A What does she look like?

B I don't know.

C Is she tall?

D Does he have glasses?

E Yes, he does.

Listen again and practice.

Talk Some More Write the words in the correct spaces.

is	has
what	isn't
I	friend
does	have

Do you know my ________ Paul?

I'm not sure. ________ does he look like?

He ________ blond, curly hair.

________ he tall?

No, he ________. He's kind of average height.

Does he ________ glasses?

Yes, he ________.

Oh, yeah. ________ know him.

Check your answers.

Practice the conversation with a partner. Use information about your own friend.

Work In Pairs Ask your partner questions. Fill in the missing information. Find Dave and Sally.

Student A

Student B ☞ go to page 83.

	IS	HAS
Dave	tall	________, ________ hair ________
Sally	________	long, curly hair earrings

Speak Out

Work in groups. Think of a person in your class. Your classmates will ask questions and guess the person. Only answer the questions if they begin with *Is...?* or *Does...?*

ZOOM IN

In many cultures, people are interested in other people's age. In some cultures, it's very rude to ask a person's age, but it's normal in others.

How about in your culture? Is it OK to ask adults their age? Does it make any difference whether they're men or women? How about children?

UNIT 4

GOALS

Do you speak English?

- Asking for and offering help
- Thanking people
- Describing locations

Get Ready **Look at the picture. Write the words in the correct spaces.**

between | in front of | behind | next to

The First Trust Bank is __________ the department store.

The subway station is __________ the Royal Hotel and the police station.

The bus stop is __________ the post office.

The movie theater is __________ the department store.

Start Talking **Look at the conversation above.**

Practice with a partner. Take turns asking about other places above.

Listen In

Listen and write the number of the conversation next to each sentence (1-3).

I only speak a little. ____	Thanks. ____	Sure. ____
I speak English. ____	Thank you. ____	You're welcome. ____
A little bit. ____	Thanks a lot. ____	Don't mention it. ____

Listen again and check (✓) the places the people are looking for.

Say It Right

Listen to the examples.

station	speak	help	bank

Which of the following words have the same underlined vowel sound?
Write the word in the correct column above.

that	welcome	train	please
subway	thanks	police	anyway

Listen and check your answers.

Listen again and practice.

Talk Some More

Number the conversation in the correct order (1-3).

Check your answers.

Practice the conversation with a partner. Talk about places in your city.

Work In Pairs

Ask your partner questions and mark the following places on your map.

Student A

Student B go to page 84.

hotel

bookstore

museum

Speak Out

Write the names of three places in your city or near your school. Note the locations.

PLACE	LOCATION

Work in groups. Describe the locations to your partners. Let them guess the places.

It's next to the convenience store.

ZOOM IN

What do you usually say to people in the following situations?

- when someone holds open a door for you
- when someone gives you a gift
- when someone does some work for you
- when someone lends you something

Thank you.

You're welcome.

In English, people usually just say *thank you* or *thanks*. *Thanks* is less formal than saying *thank you*. In what kinds of situations do you usually thank people in your culture?

Where are you from?

▶ Asking and answering questions about where people are from

Get Ready **Where are these people from? Match the countries and the people.**

- Brazil
- Japan
- Mexico
- Taiwan
- Canada
- Korea

Start Talking **Look at the conversation above.**

Practice with a partner. Imagine you are one of the people in the picture.

Listen In

Listen and circle the names you hear.
Write them in the chart.

Anita	Paul	Tomoko	Winston
Steve	John	Anne	Patricia

NAME	FROM?	ON VACATION?

Listen again and fill in the chart.

Say It Right

Match the countries with the same stress pattern.

1	Mex•i•co	Ma•lay•sia
2	Bra•zil	Ven•e•zue•la
3	Ko•re•a	Can•a•da
4	Eng•land	Tai•wan
5	In•do•ne•sia	Swe•den

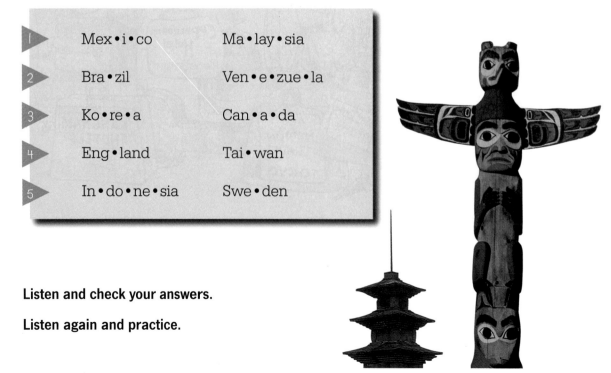

Listen and check your answers.

Listen again and practice.

Talk Some More

Match the questions and answers.

What's your name?
Where are you from?
Are you on vacation?
What do you do?
I'm a student.
Yes, I am.
Maria.
I'm from Mexico.

Check your answers.

Practice the conversation with a partner. Use your own information.

Work In Pairs

Look at the information. Fill in the chart with as much information as you can about these three women.

Student A

Student **B** ☞ go to page 85.

Mary is from Australia.

Ms. Lee isn't from Australia or Brazil.

Gina isn't from Taiwan or Australia.

Ms. Oliveira is from Brazil.

IMMIGRATION

Name	From?	Doing what?

Read your information to your partner. Listen and fill in the missing information.

Ask your partner questions to check your answers.

Speak Out

Imagine you are visiting from a foreign country. Write the country on a piece of paper. Also write whether you are a student, or on vacation.

Exchange papers. Ask questions and find the person whose paper you're holding.

ZOOM IN

When you meet a person for the first time, some questions are OK to ask, and others may not be. Which questions do you think are all right to ask? Check (✓) them.

How much money do you make?

- ☐ Where are you from?
- ☐ What's your name?
- ☐ How old are you?
- ☐ Are you married?
- ☐ Do you have any children?
- ☐ What do you do?
- ☐ How much money do you make?

Does everyone in your class agree? What other questions are OK to ask?

UNIT 6

Make yourself at home.

- Welcoming someone
- Offering, accepting, and refusing

Get Ready

Write the missing information in the correct place below.

Thanks. I like it a lot, too. | Yes, please. | Thanks.

Come in and make yourself at home.
Your new apartment is really nice.
Would you like some tea?
TEA

Check your answers.

Make a list of all the items on the table. Check with a partner.

Start Talking

Look at the conversation above.

Practice with a partner. Offer him/her something from the table above.

Would you like some juice?
No, thanks.

Listen In

Listen and check (✓) the words you hear.

☐ tea	☐ water	☐ bedroom	☐ bathroom
☐ coffee	☐ cookies	☐ living room	
☐ juice	☐ cakes	☐ kitchen	

Listen again and number the pictures (1-3).

Say It Right

Look for the letter *c* in the conversations below. Circle the ones that sound like /s/. Underline the ones that sound like /k/.

1
A Come in. Make yourself comfortable.
B Wow. This place is really nice.

2
A Would you like some juice or coffee?
B Thanks. A cup of coffee sounds great.

3
A How about some cookies?
B No, thanks. But can I have some water, please?
A Of course.

Listen and check your answers.

Listen again and practice.

Talk Some More

Number the sentences to make a conversation (1-6).

[6] Thanks a lot.

[ ] May I have some coffee, please?

[ ] Thanks. Nice place.

[1] Hi. Come in.

[ ] Sure. Here you are.

[ ] Thanks. Would you like some tea or coffee?

Check your answers.

Practice the conversation with a partner. Use your own information.

Work In Pairs

Look at the pictures and write what you think the host is saying.

Student A

Student B go to page 86.

Read the information to your partner. Let your partner find the correct match in his/her photos.

Speak Out

Make a list of items you would offer visitors to your home.

Would you like a sandwich?

Offer your classmates the items on your list. Write their names next to the things they accept. Try to write a different name for each item.

ZOOM IN

When you visit someone's home for the first time, do you like to look around? If so, you're not unusual. Most people love to see how other people live.

Is it OK if I look around?

In your culture, is it OK to ask your host to show you around?

How much is this sweater?

GOALS

- Asking about and stating prices
- Talking about forms of payment

Get Ready **Look at the advertisement. Match the names with the pictures.**

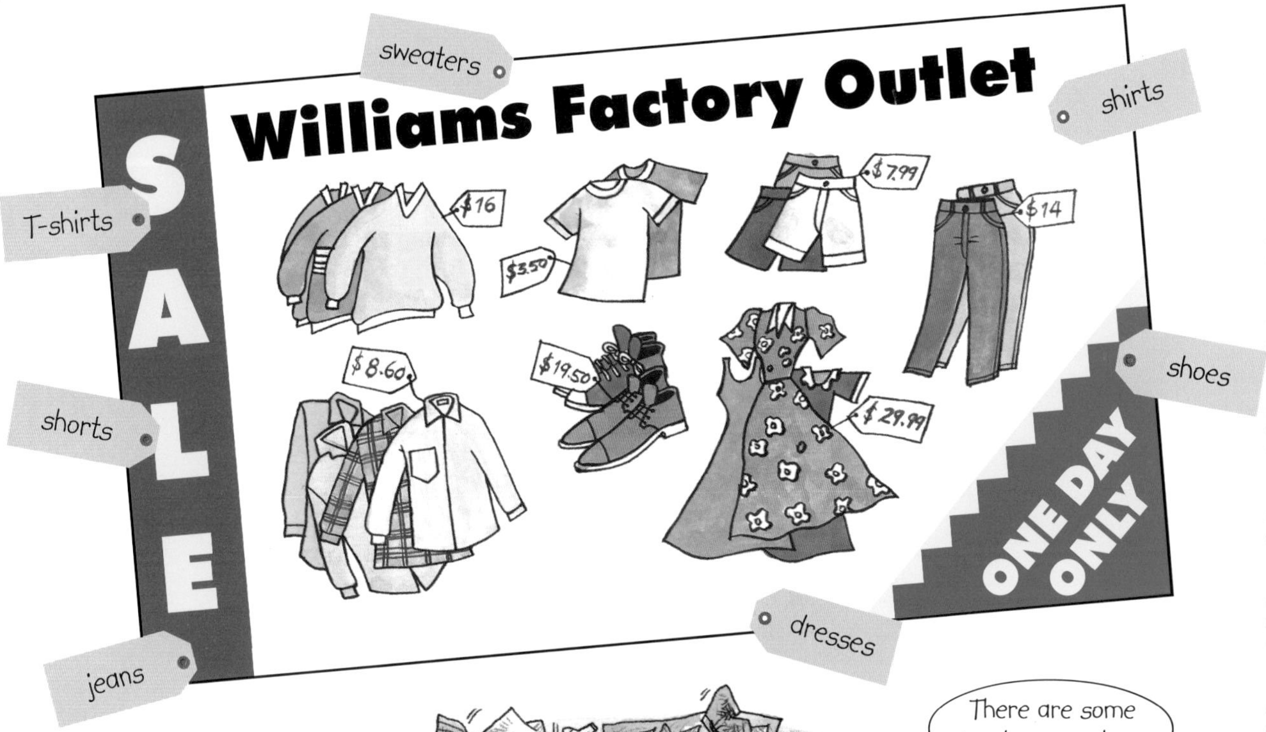

Start Talking **Look at the conversation above.**

Practice with a partner. Ask and answer questions about other items on sale.

Listen In

Listen and circle the words you hear.

How much are the shoes/sweaters?
How much are they/is it?
How many do you need/want?
What are you looking for/at?
How much is the black/red dress?
Do you take personal/traveller's checks?

Listen again and match the prices with the items.

$22.99
$2.99
$15
$4.50

$14
$40
$16
$60

Say It Right

Listen to the example.

Listen and mark the intonation.

Listen again and practice.

Talk Some More Write the words in the correct spaces.

credit cards | shoes | sorry | $35.50

I'll take the sweater and the ________.
Do you take ____________?
That'll be ________, please.
No, we don't. ________. Cash only.
WOMEN'S W

Check your answers.

Practice the conversation with a partner. Use your own information.

Work In Pairs Ask your partner questions and fill in the missing information.

Student A Student B go to page 87.

SALE
$ 4.99
$ 17.25
$ 10.95
$ 15.99
How much are the shirts?
They're $10.95.

Speak Out

Look at the items below. How much do you think they cost? Write the prices.

Item	My Price	Student 1's Price	Student 2's Price	Student 3's Price
jeans				
shirts				
shoes				
sweaters				
T-shirts				

Work in groups. First ask your partners for their prices and fill in the chart. Then choose items you want to buy and practice paying.

Who has the lowest price for jeans in your group? ____________

Who has the highest price for shoes in your group? ____________

Who has the most expensive item in your group? ____________

Who has the cheapest item in your group? ____________

Who has the best prices in your group? ____________

ZOOM IN

In certain cultures, salesclerks follow customers around closely when shopping for clothes or other items. Some customers like this attention, but others sometimes don't.

How about in your country? Do people generally like salespeople to offer them help, or would they rather seek help only when they need it?

UNIT 8

I need a part-time job.

- Expressing desires
- Making suggestions
- Talking about likes and dislikes

Get Ready **Match the occupation with the picture.**

lifeguard   movie usher   waiter   receptionist   taxi driver

Start Talking **Look at the conversation above.**

Practice with a partner.
Talk about the other occupations above.

I want to work as a lifeguard.
Why don't you try Sunshine Pools?
To Sunshine Piranha farm

Listen In

Listen and circle the occupations you hear.

I get to meet lots of people.

I can drive.

Try Sunshine Pools.

I have to work nights.

Listen again and match the occupation with the sentence you hear.

Say It Right

Listen to the example.

I need a part-time job.

Which sentences have the same stress pattern as the example? Check (✓) them.

1. ☐ I need to earn some cash.
2. ☐ I want an interesting job.
3. ☐ I like to work at night.
4. ☐ I want to drive a cab.
5. ☐ I want to be a lifeguard.

Listen and check your answers.

Listen again and practice.

Talk Some More

Write the words in the correct spaces.

like | part-time | yes | usher | see

Do you have a __________ job?
Yes, I'm an __________.
Do you ______ it?
______, I do.
Why?
I get to ______ lots of movies.

Check your answers.

Practice the conversation with a partner. Talk about other occupations.

Work In Pairs

Ask your partner questions and fill in the missing information.

Does Bill have a part-time job?
Yes, he's a taxi driver.

Student A Student B ☞ go to page 88.

NAME	JOB	LIKE IT?	WHY/WHY NOT?
Bill		☺	loves driving
Jenny			
Amy		☺	loves swimming
Shawn			
Thomas		☺	meets lots of people

Speak Out

What do you want to do? Read the information and circle the right answers for you.

Do you want to ...

	YOU	YOUR PARTNER
work nights?	yes / no	yes / no
work outdoors?	yes / no	yes / no
drive a car?	yes / no	yes / no
work in an office?	yes / no	yes / no
use a computer?	yes / no	yes / no
work alone?	yes / no	yes / no

Why don't you try working as a house painter?

Ask a partner and circle his/her answers.

Suggest a job for your partner.

ZOOM IN

Different cultures have different rules about the use of special titles when talking about employees. In some cultures, a person's level in their office is used as a title, such as *president* or *department head*. In other cultures, the name of the occupation is more common, such as *architect* or *attorney*. In most English-speaking cultures, *professor* and *doctor* are the only special titles used. Otherwise, people are simply called *Mr.*, *Mrs.* or *Ms.*

You're coming with us, Mister!
That's Professor to you!

How about in your culture? Do you use special titles when talking about people's occupations?

GOALS

Is there a pool?

- Asking for and identifying locations in a building
- Giving directions

Get Ready **Match the name with the correct place in the hotel.**

THIRD FLOOR
SECOND FLOOR
FIRST FLOOR
WASH
Excuse me.
Yes, Sir?
Is there a business center in this hotel?
Yes, there is. It's on the second floor next to the restaurant.

- pool
- front desk
- business center
- newsstand
- restaurant
- laundry
- health club
- coffee shop

Start Talking **Look at the conversation above.**

Practice with a partner. Take turns asking about the other facilities in the hotel.

Listen In

Listen and write the number of the conversation next to the facilities you hear (1-4).

Listen again and match the place with the directions.

- Take the elevator to the second floor. Turn left, and you'll find it next to the business center.
- Just go down those stairs right there and turn right.
- Take the elevator to the third floor and turn to your left.
- Go up the stairs and turn right.

Say It Right

Listen to the examples. What is more important – the facility, or where it is?

	FACILITY	WHERE?
Example 1	✓	
Example 2		✓

Listen and check (✓) the correct column.

	FACILITY	WHERE?
1		
2		
3		
4		
5		
6		

Listen again and check your answers.

Talk Some More

Look at the hotel at the beginning of this unit. Fill in the missing information.

____________________.
____________ health club in this hotel?
How do I get there?
Yes, ma'am?
Yes, ____________.
Take the elevator to the third floor. It's ________________.

Check your answers.

Practice the conversation with a partner. Then make up your own conversation using the hotel at the beginning of this unit.

Work In Pairs

Take turns asking and answering questions about the hotels. How many differences can you find?

Student A

Student B go to page 89.

LAUNDRY
HOTEL
Is there a business center in this hotel?
Yes, there is.
Where is it?
BUSINESS CENTER
Coffee Shop
HEALTH CLUB
NEWSSTAND

Speak Out

What facilities do you want in a hotel?
Circle the right answer for you.

Do you want a ...

	YOU	YOUR PARTNER
health club?	yes / no	yes / no
restaurant?	yes / no	yes / no
coffee shop?	yes / no	yes / no
business center?	yes / no	yes / no
pool?	yes / no	yes / no
laundry?	yes / no	yes / no

I want a health club because I like to exercise a lot.

Ask a partner and circle his/her answers.

Give reasons for your answers.

ZOOM IN

In some cultures, the idea of numbered street addresses is unfamiliar. In these cultures, people are often very good at identifying locations and giving directions. For example, in a huge city like Tokyo, people can give instructions on how to get across town and find a particular location.

Well, you take the subway to Shinjuku Station. Take Exit 28C, turn right and walk for three blocks. You will see a police box. Turn left and walk two more blocks. On your left you will see a large blue building. Make another left, and walk one more block. Right in front of you will be a small coffee shop called Coffee Time. I'll meet you there.

GOALS

First, you turn it on.

- Describing procedures
- Narrating a sequence

Get Ready

Write the number next to the correct item (1-6).

1. fax machine
2. cassette player
3. CD player
4. answering machine
5. computer
6. VCR

Start Talking

Look at the conversation above.

Practice with a partner. Talk about other items in the picture above.

Listen In

Listen and check (✓) the words you hear in each conversation.

INSTRUCTIONS	1	2	3	4
plug in	____	____	____	____
turn on	____	____	____	____
open	____	____	____	____
press	____	____	____	____
put in	____	____	____	____
click on	____	____	____	____
take out	____	____	____	____
turn off	____	____	____	____

Listen again. Which item is each person giving instructions for? Number the items (1-4).

☐ computer

☐ VCR

☐ cassette player

☐ answering machine

☐ fax machine

☐ coffee maker

☐ CD player

Say It Right

Underline the words with the same sound as *s* in *cassette.* Circle the words with the same sound as *sh* in *shirt.*

First, make sure the cord is plugged in. Next, press the *on* switch. Then, you should push this button. Now, sit back and enjoy the show. That's all. It's simple.

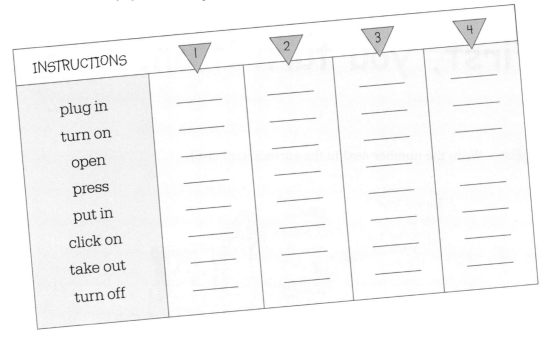

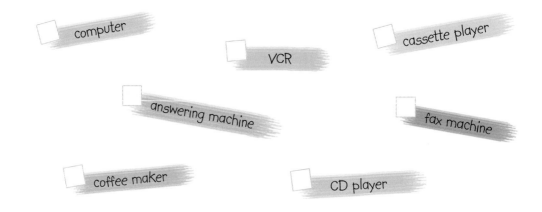

Listen and check your answers.

Listen again and practice.

Talk Some More

Write the words in the correct spaces.

press | put in | sit back | turn on | plug in | press

I can't __________ the VCR.

Well, first you need to __________ the cord.

Oh, OK.

Then, you have to __________ the *on* button.

All right.

Now, __________ the video tape.

Uh-huh.

Finally, __________ the *play* button.

OK. Now what?

Now, __________ and enjoy the show.

Check your answers.

Practice the conversation with a partner. Talk about other items.

Work In Pairs

Match the instructions with the pictures. Then number the pictures in the correct order.

Student A

Student B ☞ go to page 90.

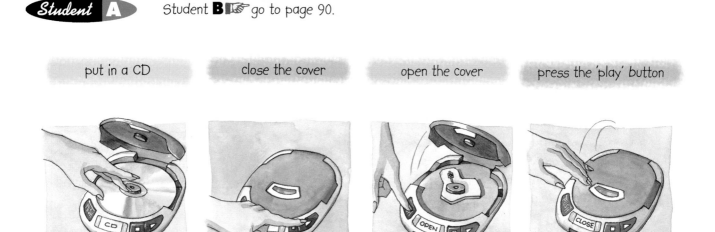

put in a CD | close the cover | open the cover | press the 'play' button

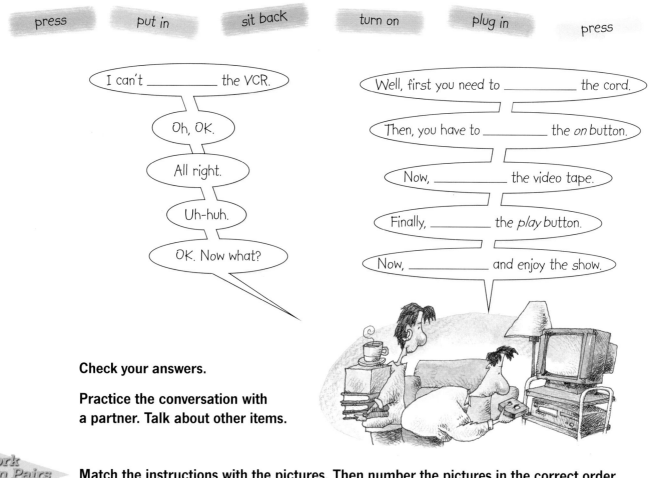

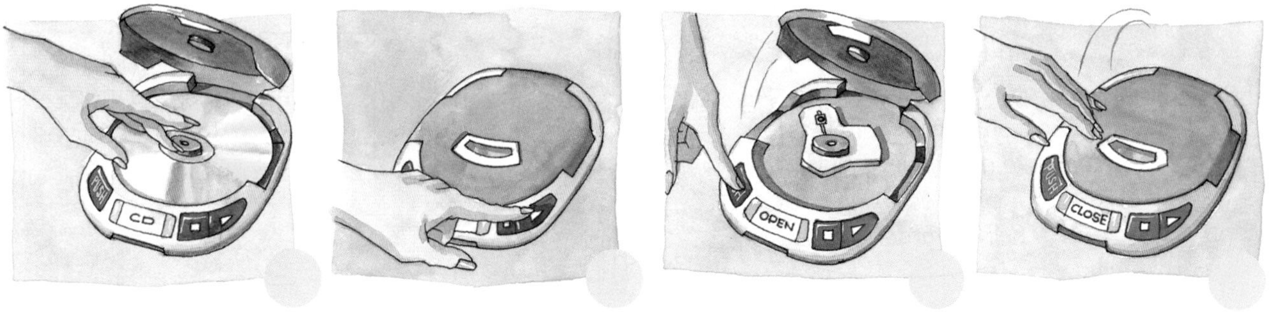

Describe the instructions to your partner. He/She will tell them to you from memory.

Speak Out

Work in groups. Choose one of the objects below. Act out the instructions. Let your partners say the name of each action.

You're making coffee!

Work in groups. Choose one of the items and make up a list of instructions for it.

How to use a ______________________

____

____

____

Compare your list with other groups. How are the lists similar/different?

ZOOM IN

Listening to instructions on the telephone can be one of the hardest tasks a student faces in a foreign language. Many companies use recorded messages on the telephone as part of their customer service program. Sometimes these messages have long or difficult instructions.

Thank you for calling Century Pizza. For restaurant locations, press 1. To hear our complete menu, press 2. For special promos, press 3. To place a delivery order, press...

What kinds of companies/services use recorded messages in your country?

GOALS

I get up early.

- Describing routines and schedules
- Telling time

Get Ready **Match the activity with the picture.**

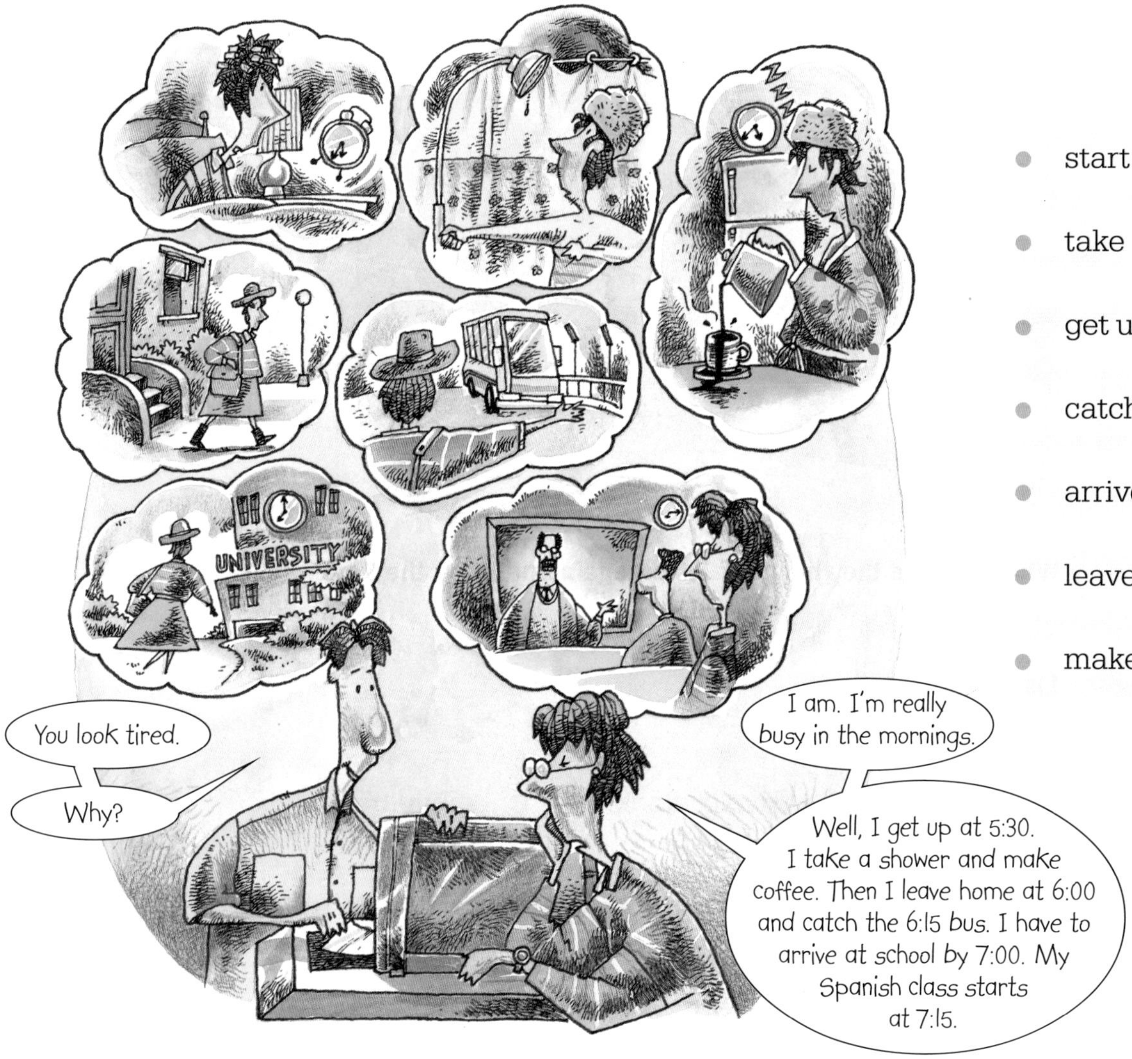

- start class
- take a shower
- get up
- catch the bus
- arrive at school
- leave home
- make coffee

Start Talking **Look at the conversation above.**

Practice with a partner. Use your own information.

Listen In

Listen and number the pictures in the correct order (1-6).

What time did they happen? Listen again and mark the time in the clocks.

Say It Right

Listen and practice.

1	Five o' clock.	Five o' clock?
2	Tired.	Tired?
3	By bus.	By bus?
4	Busy day.	Busy day?
5	Downtown.	Downtown?

Listen and circle the best response above.

Listen again and check your answers.

Talk Some More

Number the sentences to make a conversation (1-6).

- Tired? What time do you get up? [ ]
- 5:30. [ ]
- I'm tired. [ ]
- How come? [ ]
- What's the matter? [1]
- I have an early morning computer class. [6]

Check your answers.

Practice the conversation with a partner.
Use your own information, or one of these activities.

- go jogging
- walk the dog
- do homework
- check e-mail

Work In Pairs

Ask your partner questions and fill in the missing information.

Student A Student **B** go to page 91.

	gets up	has breakfast	goes to work	comes home	has dinner	goes to bed
Matt	6:30 am	______	7:45 am	______	7:00 pm	______
Andrew	______	5:30 pm	______	5:15 am	______	10:00 am

What time does he get up?

What kind of work do you think Andrew does?

Speak Out

Survey three of your classmates.

Find out what time they...

	Student 1	Student 2	Student 3
get up			
have breakfast			
leave home			
arrive at work or school			
have lunch			
go home			
have dinner			
watch TV			
go to bed			

Alice goes to bed at 1:00.

Share your information with a partner. Then answer these questions. Ask the people to give reasons.

Who gets up the earliest in your class? ____________

Who gets up the latest? ____________

Who goes to bed the earliest? ____________

Who goes to bed the latest? ____________

ZOOM IN

In some cultures it is important to be on time for social events. In other cultures it's all right to arrive late. How about in your culture? How late can you be for a dinner invitation or a party? Is it the same for men and women? Teenagers and adults?

Oh, sorry I'm late.

Do you have to apologize if you're late?

GOALS

I'd like a hamburger.

- Ordering food and drink
- Asking for additional information

Get Ready **Write the number next to the correct item (1-10).**

Can I help you?
I'd like a hamburger and a medium iced tea, please.
Is that all?
Yes, thanks.

1. hamburger
2. pizza
3. fries
4. salad
5. chicken
6. hot dog
7. soda
8. iced tea
9. mustard
10. ketchup

Start Talking **Look at the conversation above.**

Practice with a partner. Order items that you like.

Listen In

Listen and check (✓) these words every time you hear them.

☐ hamburger	☐ salad	☐ soda	☐ mustard	☐ small
☐ fries	☐ pizza	☐ coffee	☐ ketchup	☐ medium
☐ chicken	☐ hot dog	☐ iced tea	☐ napkins	☐ large

Listen again and take the orders.

Say It Right

Do the words end in /s/ or /z/? Check (✓) the column.

		/s/	/z/
1	drinks	____	____
2	hamburgers	____	____
3	hot dogs	____	____
4	thanks	____	____
5	napkins	____	____

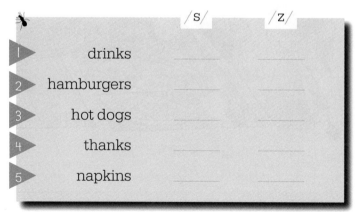

Listen and check your answers.

Listen again and practice.

Talk Some More

Number the sentences to make a conversation (1-6).

Yes. Can I have a hamburger, please?
Yes. And a soda, please.
Medium.
What size?
1
Can I help you?
Would you like ketchup and mustard on that?

Check your answers.

Practice the conversation with a partner. Use your own information.

Work In Pairs

Look at the menu and order food from your partner.

Student A

Student B go to page 92.

HAMBURGER WIZARD
Hamburger
Cheeseburger
Hot dog
Chicken Sandwich
French Fries
Soft Drinks
Iced Tea
Is that all?
MENU

Speak Out

Choose a type of restaurant and create a menu with a partner.

Work with another partner.
Show your partner the menu and take his/her order.

ZOOM IN

In some cultures, people often make special requests when ordering food in restaurants. In other cultures, however, people only order items exactly as they appear on the menu. Which way do you prefer?

Yes, I'd like the chef's salad, but without the tomatoes. Could I substitute extra cucumbers? Great. Then I'd like extra croutons, and I'll have ranch dressing, but put it on the side. Make sure it's the fat free one! And could I have some parmesan cheese with that? But make sure it's the real cheese, not that stuff in a can...
REAL FAST FOOD

How about in your culture? Do many people give special instructions when ordering food?

GOALS
- Talking about likes and dislikes
- Describing sports

Do you like basketball?

Get Ready **Write the number next to the correct picture (1-10).**

1. basketball
2. gymnastics
3. soccer
4. diving
5. tennis
6. golf
7. swimming
8. skiing
9. hockey
10. baseball

Start Talking **Look at the conversation above.**

Practice with a partner. Talk about the sports above.

Talk Some More

Listen and circle the sports you hear.

- exciting
- interesting
- boring
- fun

Listen again and match the words with the sports.

Say It Right

Circle the stressed syllable of each word in bold.

1. **Bas • ket • ball** is **ex • cit • ing** to watch.
2. He thinks **ski • ing** is **bor • ing**.
3. **Gym • nas • tics** is an **in • ter • est • ing** sport.

Listen and check your answers.

Listen again and practice.

Talk Some More

Write the words in the correct spaces.

exciting | what | boring | don't | like | do

Do you ________ soccer?
________ sports ________ you like?
No, I ________. It's kind of ________.
I like tennis. It's ________.

Check your answers.

Practice the conversation with a partner. Use your own information.

Work In Pairs

What do Anna and Rick think of the following sports? Ask questions and fill in the missing information.

Student A

Student B ☞ go to page 93.

	Rick	Anna
golf		boring
baseball	fun	
tennis		exciting
hockey	boring	

Does Rick like golf?

Which channel should Anna and Rick watch?

	STV	ACTION NETWORK	SPORTSNET	NOW TV
3:00	PGA Golf Highlights	World Series Game 4	NHL Game of the Week	French Open Tennis

Speak Out

Ask your classmates questions and fill in the blanks.

SPORT	NAME	COMMENT
basketball		
soccer		
tennis		
golf		
swimming		
skiing		
hockey		
baseball		
gymnastics		
diving		

Do you like basketball?
Yes, I do. It's exciting.
zzzzzzzzz

Work in groups. Answer the questions.

Which sports do most people in your class like? ______

Which sports do most people in your class dislike? ______

Which sports do you only like to watch? ______

Which sports do you only like to play? ______

ZOOM IN

Sports is a popular topic of conversation in many cultures. Many people use the topic to greet a friend or co-worker, or even to make small talk with a complete stranger.

Did you see the hockey game last night?

How about in your culture? Do people often talk about sports? Which sports? Is the same interest shared by both men and women?

GOALS

- Inviting
- Making excuses

Do you want to see a movie?

Get Ready

What kinds of movies are these? Write the name in the correct column.

Science fiction	Comedies	Thrillers	Dramas	Action films

Add another movie title to each column above.

Start Talking

Look at the conversation above.

Practice with a partner. Talk about other movies.

Listen In

Listen and match the theater with the type of movie.

- I'm going out with Judy.
- I have to study.
- I have to work late.
- I'm going to the ball game.

Listen again and match the type of movie with the excuse.

Say It Right

Listen to the intonation and check (✓) the responses that show *surprise.*

1. ☐ You do? That's too bad.
2. ☐ You are, huh? Well, maybe next time.
3. ☐ You can't? Oh, that's too bad.
4. ☐ He is? I didn't know that.
5. ☐ She can't. She has to study.

Listen again and practice.

Talk Some More

Number the sentences to make a conversation (1-6).

6 Oh, no. I forgot. I have to work late tonight.

☐ Hi, Pete.

☐ Do you want to go to a concert tonight?

☐ Who's playing?

☐ The Screamers.

1 Hello, Carol.

Check your answers.

Practice the conversation with a partner. Use your own information.

Work In Pairs

You and your partner want to see a movie with your friends. Ask questions and decide the best time to go. (When are most people free?)

Student A Student **B** go to page 94.

	BOB	KAREN	PHILIP	JOAN
FRIDAY EVENING	work late		free	
SATURDAY AFTERNOON		free		take car to garage
SATURDAY EVENING	meet boss at airport		free	
SUNDAY AFTERNOON		go shopping		bake cookies
SUNDAY EVENING	prepare for meeting on Monday		free	

How about Friday evening?
Bob has to work late Friday evening.

Speak Out

Make a note of the things you have to do this week. Leave two spaces free.

	MONDAY	TUESDAY	WEDNESDAY	THURSDAY	FRIDAY
afternoon					
evening					

Work in groups. Talk to your partners and arrange a time to see a movie.

What movie are you going to see?

____

ZOOM IN

In some cultures, if someone invites you out but you can't go (or you don't want to go), you should give a reason why. If you're doing something you *want* to do, you can say *I'm....* If it's something you *don't* really want to do, you can say *I have to....*

How about a movie?
I'm sorry. I'm going to a fashion show.
I'm sorry. I have to study for a test.

How about in your culture? Do you have to give a reason or not?

GOALS

What's the weather like?

- Talking about the weather
- Making suggestions

Get Ready **Write the words in the correct spaces below.**

hot snowy cold sunny rainy cloudy fine

What's the weather like there?
Oh, really? It's cold and snowy here.
It's hot and sunny.

Start Talking **Look at the conversation above.**

Practice with a partner. Imagine you are two of the people above.

Listen In

Listen to the weather reports. Which ones describe the weather *now?* Which ones give a *forecast?* Circle *yes* or *no.*

	1	2	3	4
NOW	yes / no	yes / no	yes / no	yes / no
FORECAST	yes / no	yes / no	yes / no	yes / no

Listen again. Check (✓) the words you hear in each report.

	1	2	3	4
hot	___	___	___	___
cold	___	___	___	___
rainy	___	___	___	___
fine	___	___	___	___
snowy	___	___	___	___
sunny	___	___	___	___
cloudy	___	___	___	___

Say It Right

Listen to the examples. Which is more important – the weather or the time?

	WEATHER	TIME
Example 1	✓	
Example 2		✓

	WEATHER	TIME
1	___	___
2	___	___
3	___	___
4	___	___
5	___	___

Listen and check (✓) the column.

Listen again and check your answers.

Talk Some More

Write the words in the correct spaces.

tomorrow | OK | what's | hot and sunny

Let's go on a picnic ________.

________ the weather going to be like?

It's going to be ________.

______. That sounds like a good idea.

Check your answers.

Practice the conversation with a partner. Use your own information.

Work In Pairs

Suggest the following activities to your partner.

Student A

Student B ☞ go to page 95.

THURSDAY	FRIDAY	SATURDAY	SUNDAY
Baseball: Sluggers play against the Swingers at Laredo open-air stadium. 7:00 pm	**Outdoor Concert:** Whispering Children on tour. At the Music Hall. 8:00 pm	**Movies:** *Ships on the Horizon* opens at the Bel-Air Cinema. 7:15 & 9:15 pm	**Garden Shows:** Rose exhibit at the Cultural Center Park. One day only. 10:00 am - 8:00 pm

Let's go to the beach on Saturday.
I don't think it's a good idea.

Speak Out

Write weather forecasts for your city.

WEATHER FORECAST Tomorrow	WEATHER FORECAST Next Month	WEATHER FORECAST In Six Months

Work in groups. Take turns reading one of your forecasts. The group will guess which one it is.

It'll be hot and sunny.

ZOOM IN

In many cultures, the weather is a popular topic of conversation. Often people use the topic in small talk, whether they're really interested in the weather or not. Why do you think this is?

Lovely weather, isn't it?

How about in your culture? Do people often talk about the weather?

GOALS

What can we get him?

- Talking about what people like
- Talking about gift giving

Get Ready **Match the statements and the pictures.**

Let's buy him a ticket to San Francisco.

How about getting him some chocolates?

Let's get him a tennis racket.

He likes reading.

He loves flowers.

He likes music.

CHOCOLATE
Max is leaving on Friday. What can we get him?
I don't know. What does he like?
Well, he likes music. Let's get him a CD.
Great idea. I'm sure he'll like that.

Start Talking **Look at the conversation above.**

Practice with a partner. Use other information above.

Listen In

Listen and write each person's likes/interests.

NAME	LIKES / INTERESTS	SUGGESTED GIFT
Julian		
Annie		
John		
Sandy		

Listen again and write the gifts the people suggest. Then choose the best gift below for each person.

____

____

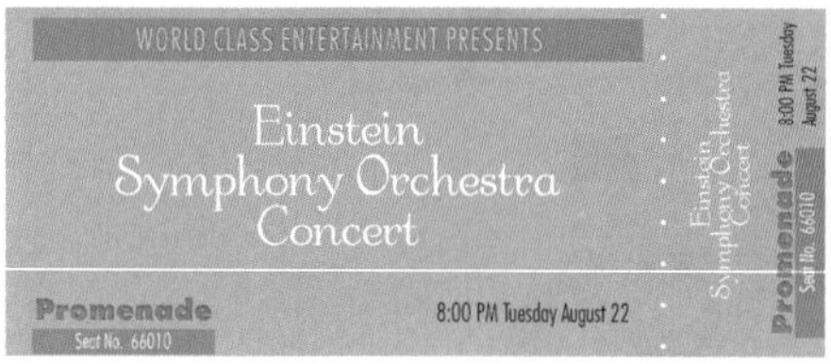

____

____

Say It Right

Listen and check (✓) the question you hear.

1	☐	What's he like?	☐	What does he like?
2	☐	What's he like?	☐	What does he like?
3	☐	What's she like?	☐	What does she like?
4	☐	What's she like?	☐	What does she like?
5	☐	What's she like?	☐	What does she like?

Listen to the questions again and practice.

Talk Some More

Write the words in the correct spaces.

Check your answers.

Practice the conversation with a partner. Use information about other people you know.

Work In Pairs

Answer your partner's questions about Bill. Decide which suggestions are good. Choose a gift for Bill.

Student A

Student B go to page 96.

Bill likes...

He already has a lot of...

cookbooks

tennis balls

videos

Ask your partner and note what Connie likes. Then suggest some gifts for her. Choose a gift for Connie.

Connie likes...

HOBBIES	SUGGESTIONS

Share your answers with the class. Who has the most original gifts?

Speak Out

Write three hobbies or activities that you like.

What do you like doing?

Work in groups. Ask your partners what they like to do. Decide the best gift for each person.

Which gift was the best for you?

ZOOM IN

Gift giving is an important custom in most cultures. Each culture has its own tradition regarding...

- the occasion when you should give a gift;
- what to give;
- what to do and say when you get a gift.

Oh, you shouldn't have!
Oh, how sweet of you!

In some cultures it's OK to open the gift right away, but in other cultures it's impolite. How about in your culture?

UNIT 17

We should go to the beach.

- Making suggestions
- Voicing objections

Get Ready **Match the words and the pictures.**

It's too hot.

It's too expensive.

It's too far.

I don't like hiking.

We don't speak Spanish.

Start Talking **Look at the conversation above.**

Practice with a partner. Talk about other places in the picture.

Listen In

Listen and write the names of the places Rick suggests.

PLACE	THINGS TO DO	OBJECTION
	hiking	too expensive
	temples, markets	don't speak Spanish
	museums, food, nightclubs	too far
	galleries, shopping	don't like hiking

Listen again and match the places, things to do, and objections.

Say It Right

Listen and circle the word you hear.

1. I can / can't swim.
2. I can / can't go in July.
3. We can / can't afford it.
4. They can / can't speak Spanish.
5. She can / can't meet us at Christmas.

Listen and check your answers.

Listen again and practice.

Talk Some More

Number the sentences to make a conversation (1-5).

- [5] But I don't like swimming.
- [ ] I think we should go to the beach.
- [ ] What can we do there?
- [ ] We can go swimming.
- [1] Where should we go on vacation?

Check your answers.

Practice the conversation with a partner.
Suggest your own place to go.

Work In Pairs

Look at the brochure and suggest a vacation in Singapore to your partner.

Student A Student B go to page 97.

SINGAPORE

Enjoy exotic flavors from a variety of cultures

Botanical gardens delight visitors all year long

Visit the Night Safari for a close-up view of the animal kingdom

Orchard Road – a shopper's paradise known around the world

Your partner has some information about Italy. Ask what you can do there.
Say which suggestions you like, which ones you don't like, and why.

Decide where you're going to go and what you're going to do.

Speak Out

Work in groups. Choose a vacation spot in your country. Brainstorm a list of things to do and see there.

Destination	Activities

Talk to students from other groups. Try to convince them to come to your vacation spot.

You should come to Sydney.

Which spot was the most popular in your class? ____________

ZOOM IN

In English there is a proverb: "All work and no play makes Jack a dull boy." In other words, people shouldn't spend 100% of their time working. Everyone deserves to take a break from time to time. Is there a similar proverb or saying in your culture? Different cultures have different attitudes about the amount of vacation time people have every year.

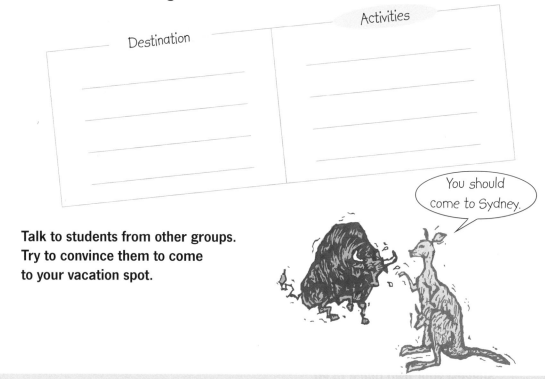

I really want to go visit my parents.

How about in your culture? How much vacation time do people usually have every year? What do you usually do?
ALOHA

What's she like?

- Describing qualities of people and jobs
- Using degrees of description

Get Ready

The scrambled words below describe people's personal qualities. Unscramble the adjectives.

Start Talking

Look at the conversation above.

Practice with a partner. Talk about other people in the picture.

Listen In

Listen. Who are they talking about? Number the pictures (1-4).

☐ 

☐ 

☐ 

☐ 

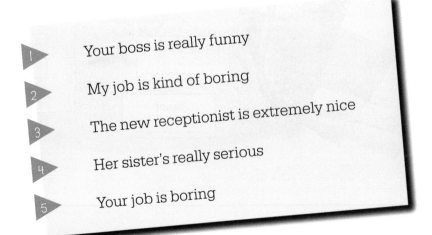

- nice
- friendly
- interesting
- serious
- funny
- hardworking

Listen again and match the people with the descriptions.

Say It Right

Listen. Are these questions or statements? Write the correct punctuation.

1. Your boss is really funny
2. My job is kind of boring
3. The new receptionist is extremely nice
4. Her sister's really serious
5. Your job is boring

Listen again and practice.

Talk Some More

Write the words in the correct spaces in the conversation.

- Kind of serious
- really nice
- really friendly
- very funny

So, how's the new job?

It's ____________. I just met Larry. He seems ____________.

Oh no! He's ____________. He makes us laugh all the time!

Really? How about Jim, the mechanic?

He's ____________.

Great! I think I'll go say 'hello.'

Check your answers.

Practice the conversation with a partner. Talk about other people you know.

Work In Pairs

You and your partner started working in the same office recently. Talk about the people you've met.

Student A

Student B ☞ go to page 98.

What words would you use to describe these people? Does your partner agree?

Speak Out

How would you describe...

your boss?

a brother or sister?

your best friend?

your job?

learning English?

Use these words, or any others you know.

very really kind of not very	nice friendly interesting serious funny hardworking boring

Work in groups. Share your information with your partners. How many similarities did you find?

ZOOM IN

"Don't judge a book by its cover." This popular expression means that a person's real qualities cannot always be known simply by their appearance.

The new boss is really nice.

Do you believe this is true? Do you have a similar expression in your culture?

UNIT 19

GOALS

What do you think of the class?

- Asking about opinions
- Expressing preferences
- Agreeing and disagreeing

Get Ready **Match the pictures and the sentences.**

GROUPA
GRAMMAR
What do you think of the class?
I do too.
It's great. I like role plays and group work a lot.

- I like role plays.
- I like listening lessons.
- I like group work.
- I like to study grammar books.
- I like to study by myself.
- I like the teacher to explain everything.
- I like to practice outside of class.

Start Talking **Look at the conversation above.**

Practice with a partner. Use the other information above.

Listen In

Listen. Do the speakers agree or disagree? Circle the correct answer.

1 agree/disagree

2 agree/disagree

3 agree/disagree

4 agree/disagree

Listen again and write the number of the conversation next to the activities you hear (1-4).

Say It Right

Listen to the example.

Listen and underline the words with the most stress.

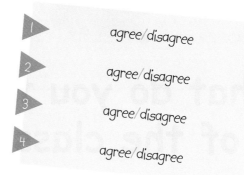

Listen again and practice.

Talk Some More

Number the sentences to make a conversation (1-5).

[ ] Really? What do you like?

[5] I like studying by myself.

[1] What do you think of the class?

[ ] It's OK. I like group work.

[ ] You do? Not me.

Check your answers.

Practice the conversation with a partner. Use your own information.

Work In Pairs

Exchange information and fill in the chart. Which students are similar to each other?

Student A Student B go to page 99.

	LIKES...	DISLIKES...
Vera	learning by reading having her own textbook studying grammar	
Erik		studying grammar studying alone writing things down
Carla	talking to native speakers watching films and videos listening	
Tony		role plays group work playing games

How does Vera like to learn?

Which student is the most like you? Which student is the least like you?

Speak Out

Write down your five favorite ways to learn English.

MY FAVORITE WAYS	AGREES	DISAGREES

Find someone in your class who agrees and someone who disagrees with each choice. Write their names.

I like to study alone.

ZOOM IN

Do you always say what you think, or do you say what you think other people want to hear? Different cultures have different attitudes about this. In some cultures it is rude to refuse a request. Instead of saying *no*, people say *maybe*.

Have some more cake.
Maybe later.

What do you say when you don't want to offend someone?

I lost my cell phone.

GOALS

- Talking about what you did and who you met
- Asking about past events

Get Ready **Match the pictures and the errands.**

- pick up credit card
- pick up shirts
- work out
- have lunch with Cindy
- buy flowers for Mom

Oh, no! I lost my cell phone.
Oh, that's terrible, Greg! Where did you go today?
Well, first I went to the dry cleaners. Then I went to the bank. Next I had lunch with my girlfriend...
WORLD OF SPORTS

Where did Greg go today?

Start Talking **Look at the conversation above.**

Practice with a partner.
Talk about the other places above.

Listen In

Listen and circle the things Greg did.

- picked up credit card
- bought chocolates
- picked up shirts
- bought flowers
- worked out at the gym
- had a hamburger
- picked up ATM card
- had pizza
- picked up pants
- bought workout clothes

Listen again and number the places in the order you hear them (1-5).

Say It Right

Circle the word with the different vowel sound in each group.

1	lost	bought	saw	shut
2	picked up	went	said	left
3	lay	ate	called	made
4	put	found	took	looked

Listen and check your answers.

Listen again and practice.

Talk Some More **Fill in the missing information.**

So, Greg, how was your day?

It was busy. I went to the bank.

What for?

______________________.
Then I went to the fitness center.

What did you do there?

______________________.

Uh-huh.

And then I went to Rosie's Grill for lunch.

Who did you have lunch with?

______________________.

Check your answers.

Practice the conversation with a partner. Use your own information.

Work In Pairs **Exchange information with a partner. Note what the people did and who they saw yesterday.**

Student A Student B ☞ go to page 100.

NAME	WENT	SAW
Pete	office, the movies	
Sandy		friends, family
Bill	gym, school	
Gina		cashier, doctor, nurse

Who did Pete see yesterday?

Speak Out

Make a list of the places you went and the people you talked to last weekend.

PLACES I WENT
PEOPLE I SAW

Work in groups. Take turns asking and answering about the places you went and the people you saw. How many similarities are there in your group?

Where did you go last weekend?

ZOOM IN

Recently, cell phones, faxes and e-mail have helped to increase people's social networks. Perhaps people now have the chance to speak to more people every day than they used to. Surprisingly, although we may talk to more people, the amount of actual contact we have with these people is often decreased because of the way we contact them!

Sure, we've got to get together one of these days.

How about you? Do you talk to more people, but see them less often than you used to? Do you think this trend will continue?

Language in Context

Are you Pat?	Yes, I am. No, I'm not.
Is he/she Pat?	Yes, he/she is. No, he/she isn't.

What's	your	name?
	his	
	her	

My	name is ______.
His	
Her	

From page 3.

Work In Pairs **Ask your partner for the missing names. Fill in the blanks.**

Student B

BACK ROW : ______, Edwin Sondhe, ______, Roger Walker
FRONT ROW : Stephen Lee, ______, Susan Chen

Language in Context

Are those your children?
No, they aren't.

Do you have any brothers or sisters?

Is	this that	your family?	Yes, it is. No, it isn't.
Are	these those	your children?	Yes, they are. No, they aren't.

Do you have any brothers or sisters?	Yes, I do. No, I don't.
	I have one brother and two sisters.

From page 7.

Work In Pairs

Student B

Imagine you're one of the people in this family. Answer your partner's questions.

Ask your partner questions. Draw his/her family tree.

Do you have any children?

UNIT 3

Language in Context

Do you know Amy?	Yes, I know her. No, I don't know her.

Is he/she tall?	Yes, he/she is. No, he/she isn't.

Does he/she have short hair?	Yes, he/she does. No, he/she doesn't.

What does he/she look like?	He's/She's	tall.
	He/She	has blond hair.

From page 11.

Work In Pairs **Ask and answer questions. Fill in the missing information. Find Dave and Sally.**

Student B

	IS	HAS
Dave	________	short, black hair glasses
Sally	average height	________, ________ hair ________

UNIT 4 Language in Context

Do you speak English?	Yes, I do. Yes, I speak English a little. No, I don't.

Can I help you?	Yes, please. No, thank you.

Where's the hotel, please?	It's next to the bank. Sorry, I don't know.

Thank you. Thanks. Thanks anyway.	You're welcome. Don't mention it. Sure.

From page 15.

Work In Pairs **Ask your partner questions and mark the following places on your map.**

Student B

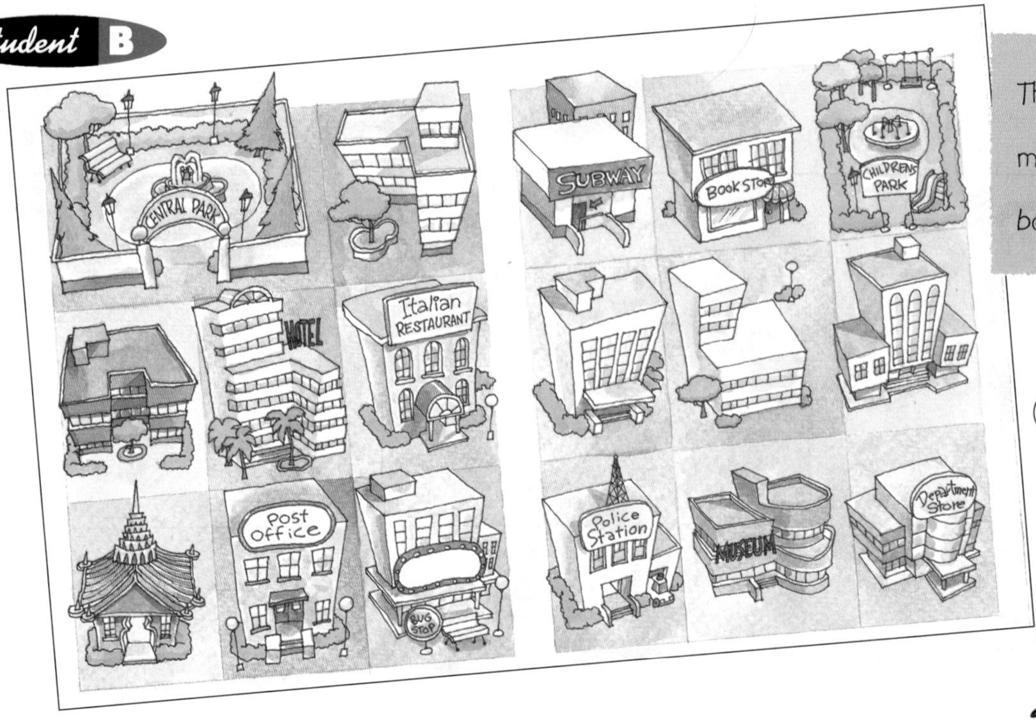

Thai restaurant

movie theater

bank

UNIT 5 Language in Context

Where are you from?	I'm from Mexico.

Are you on vacation?	Yes, I am. No, I'm not.

What do you do?	I'm a student.

From page 19.

Work In Pairs **Look at the information. Fill in the chart with as much information as you can about these three women.**

Student B

Ms. Stewart isn't from Taiwan or Brazil.

Jenny is from Taiwan.

Mary is on vacation.

Two of the people are students.

Name	From?	Doing what?

Read your information to your partner. Listen and fill in the missing information.

Ask your partner questions to check your answers.

Language in Context

Come in. Make yourself at home.	Thank you. Thanks a lot.

Would you like some coffee?	Yes, please. No, thank you.

May I have some water?	Sure. Here you are.

From page 23.

Work In Pairs **Look at the pictures and fill in what you think the guest is saying.**

Student B

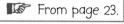

Read the information to your partner. Let your partner find the correct match in his/her photos.

Language in Context

How much	is	the sweater? it?	It's $16.
	are	the sweaters? they?	They're $16.

I'll take this shirt.	That'll be $30, please.

Do you take credit cards?	Yes, we do. No, we don't.

From page 27.

Work In Pairs **Ask your partner questions and fill in the missing information.**

Student B

SALE
$ 18.50
$ 10.95
$ 14.50
$ 8.60
How much are the shirts?
They're $10.95.

UNIT 8

Language in Context

I need a part-time job.	Why don't you try Sunshine Pools?

What kind of job do you want?	I want to work as a lifeguard.

Do you have a job?	Yes, I'm a waiter. No, I don't.

From page 31.

Work In Pairs

Ask your partner questions and fill in the missing information.

Student B

NAME	JOB	LIKE IT?	WHY/WHY NOT?
Bill		☺	loves driving
Jenny		☹	has a terrible boss
Amy			
Shawn		☹	has to work nights
Thomas			

UNIT 9

Language in Context

Excuse me. Is there a pool in this hotel?
Where is it?
Yes, there is.
It's on the second floor.

Excuse me.	Yes, sir? Yes, ma'am?

Is there a pool in this hotel?	Yes, there is. No, there isn't.

Where is it?	It's on the second floor.

How do I get there?	Take the stairs to the second floor. It's next to the health club.

From page 35.

Work In Pairs

Take turns asking and answering questions about the hotels. How many differences can you find?

Student B

HOTEL
LAUNDRY
NEWSSTAND
HEALTH CLUB
Coffee Shop
BUSINESS CENTER
Is there a business center in this hotel?
Yes, there is.
Where is it?

Language in Context

Do you know how to use a computer?	Yes, it's easy. No, it looks difficult.

I can't turn on the VCR.	First,	you need to plug it in.
	Then,	you have to press the *on* button.
	Finally,	press the *play* button.

From page 39.

Work In Pairs

Match the instructions with the pictures. Then number the pictures in the correct order.

Student B

dial the number | put in the paper | press the *start* button | listen for the fax tone

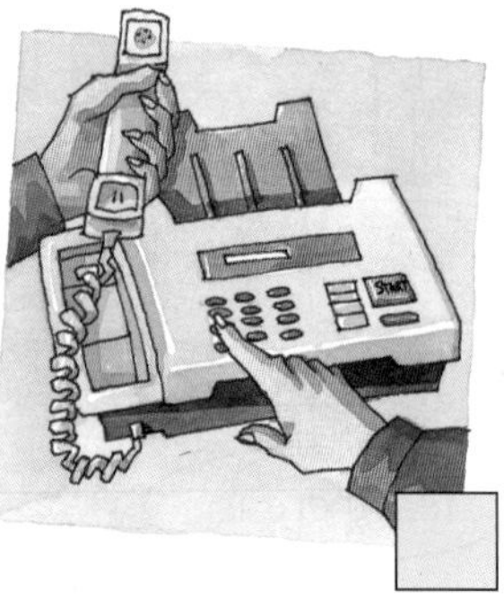

Describe the instructions to your partner. He/She will tell them to you from memory.

Language in Context

What time
do you get up?
10:30.

What's the matter?	I'm tired.

Why are you tired?	I get up at 5:30 every morning.
How come?	I have an early morning class.

What time do you get up?	At 7:00.

From page 43.

Work In Pairs **Ask your partner questions and fill in the missing information.**

Student B

	gets up	has breakfast	goes to work	comes home	has dinner	goes to bed
Matt	____	7:00 am	____	6:30 pm	____	10:30 pm
Andrew	5:00 pm	____	6:00 pm	____	6:30 am	____

What time does
he get up?

What kind of work do you think Andrew does?

UNIT 12

Language in Context

Can I help you?	I'd like a hamburger, please. No, thanks.

What size would you like?	Medium, please.

Is that all?	Yes, thanks. No, I'd also like an iced tea.

Would you like ketchup on that?	Yes, please. No, thanks.

From page 47.

Work In Pairs **Listen to your partner's order. Ask questions and mark the order form.**

Student B

HAMBURGER WIZARD
ORDER FORM

Hamburger	regular	.70	☐	double	1.20	☐		
Cheeseburger	regular	.90	☐	double	1.40	☐		
Hot dog	regular	.70	☐	w/ cheese	.90	☐		
Chicken Sandwich	regular	.90	☐	w/ cheese	1.10	☐		
French Fries	regular	.60	☐	large	.80	☐		
Soft Drinks	small	.60	☐	medium	.80	☐	large 1.00	☐
Iced Tea	small	.50	☐	medium	.70	☐	large .90	☐

Total $

UNIT 13 Language in Context

Do you like basketball?	Yes, I do. No, not really. No, I don't.

What sports do you like?	I like soccer. It's exciting.

From page 51.

Work In Pairs **What do Anna and Rick think of the following sports? Ask questions and fill in the missing information.**

Student B

	Rick	Anna
golf	great	
baseball		boring
tennis	interesting	
hockey		great

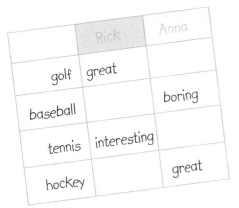

Which channel should Anna and Rick watch?

	STV	ACTION NETWORK	SPORTSNET	NOW TV
3:00	PGA Golf Highlights	World Series Game 4	NHL Game of the Week	French Open Tennis

Language in Context

Do you want to	see a movie?	Which one?
	go to a concert?	What's/Who's playing?
		That sounds good.
		Oh, no. I have to work tonight.

How about a science fiction movie?	OK.
	No, I don't like science fiction.
	Sorry, I have to work late.
	Sorry, I'm going out to dinner tonight.

From page 55.

Work In Pairs

You and your partner want to see a movie with your friends. Ask questions and decide the best time to go. (When are the most people free?)

Student B

	BOB	KAREN	PHILIP	JOAN
FRIDAY EVENING		clean apartment		free
SATURDAY AFTERNOON	go to meeting		play tennis	
SATURDAY EVENING		visit aunt in hospital		go to concert
SUNDAY AFTERNOON	free		study for exam	
SUNDAY EVENING		free		free

How about Friday evening?
Karen has to clean her apartment Friday evening.

UNIT 15

Language in Context

What's the weather like?	It's cold and snowy.

Let's go on a picnic tomorrow.	OK. That sounds like a good idea. I don't think it's a good idea.

What's the weather going to be like? What's the weather forecast?	It's going to be hot and sunny.

From page 59.

Work In Pairs Listen to your partner's suggestions. Look at the weather forecast and give answers.

Student B

UNIT 16 Language in Context

What can we get him/her?	Let's get him/her a CD.	Great idea. I'm sure he'll/she'll like that.
	How about getting him/her a cookbook?	No, he/she already has a lot of cookbooks.

What does he/she like? What do you like doing?	He likes music. I like cooking.

From page 63.

Work In Pairs

Ask your partner and note what Bill likes. Then suggest some gifts for him. Choose a gift for Bill.

Student B

Bill likes...

HOBBIES	SUGGESTIONS

Answer your partner's questions about Connie. Decide which sugestions are good. Choose a gift for Connie.

Connie likes...

She already has a lot of...
workout clothes
art books
classical music CDs

Share your answers with the class. Who has the most original gifts?

UNIT 17

Language in Context

Where should we go on vacation?	I think we should go to the beach.	It's too hot.
What can we do there?	We can go swimming.	I don't like swimming.

From page 67.

Work In Pairs

Look at the brochure and suggest a vacation in Italy to your partner.

Student B

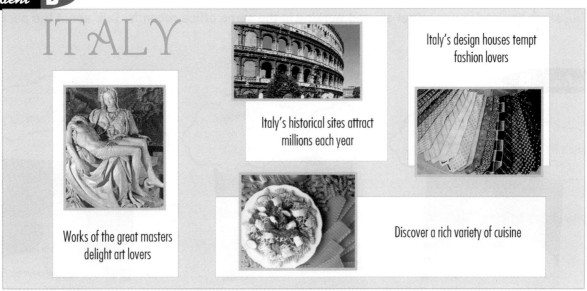

ITALY

Italy's historical sites attract millions each year

Italy's design houses tempt fashion lovers

Works of the great masters delight art lovers

Discover a rich variety of cuisine

Your partner has some information about Singapore. Ask what you can do there. Say which suggestions you like, which ones you don't like, and why.

Decide where you're going to go and what you're going to do.

UNIT 18 Language in Context

What's he/she like?	He's/She's	very really kind of not very	nice.
How's your new job?	It's		interesting.

Did you meet the new cashier?	Yes, I did. No, I didn't.

☞ From page 71.

Work In Pairs

You and your partner started working in the same office recently. Talk about the people you've met.

Student B

What words would you use to describe these people? Does your partner agree?

UNIT 19 Language in Context

What do you think of the class?	It's great. It's OK.

I like role plays.	I do too. Me too.
I like studying alone.	I don't. Not me.

From page 75.

Work In Pairs **Exchange information and fill in the chart. Which students are similar to each other?**

Student B

	LIKES...	DISLIKES...
Vera		practicing outside of class talking to native speakers group work
Erik	group work role plays practicing outside class	
Carla		the teacher explaining everything learning by reading practicing pronunciation
Tony	the teacher explaining everything having grammar lessons studying alone	

How does Vera like to learn?

Which student is the most like you? Which student is the least like you?

UNIT 20

Language in Context

I lost my glasses.
That's terrible!

I lost my cell phone.	That's terrible!

Where did you go today?
Well, first I went to the office...

Where did you go today?	First, Then, Next,	I went to the bank.

How was your day?	It was busy.

From page 79.

Work In Pairs

Exchange information with a partner. Note what the people did and who they saw yesterday.

Student B

NAME	WENT	SAW
Pete		boss, secretary, co-workers
Sandy	birthday party, lunch at Mom's	
Bill		instructor, teachers, students
Gina	supermarket, medical center	

Where did Pete go yesterday?